C A N A D I A N

# FIGHTER PILOT

*"Only the spirit of attack*

*born of a brave heart*

*will bring success to any aircraft*

*no matter how advanced it may be"*

Adolf Galland.

To:

Merrill and Lauren O'Malley

and

David "DJ" McQuarrie

# CANADIAN
# FIGHTER PILOT
## A LEGACY OF COURAGE AND DEDICATION

TEXT AND PHOTOS BY **JOHN McQUARRIE**
DESIGN BY **DAVID O'MALLEY**

Copyright:   1992 John McQuarrie

First published in 1992 by
McGraw-Hill Ryerson Limited
300 Water Street
Whitby, Ontario
L1N 9B6

Produced for McGraw-Hill Ryerson Limited by:
Image House
107 York Street
Ottawa, Canada
K1N 5T4
(613) 236-1833

Colour Separations:  Chromagraphics, Singapore
Printing and Binding:  Tien Wah Press, Singapore

**Canadian Cataloguing in Publication Data**

McQuarrie, John, 1946
Canadian fighter pilot :
a legacy of courage and dedication

ISBN 0-07-551480-X

1. Fighter pilots--Canada--Biography. 2. Canada. Royal Canadian Air Force--Biography.  3. Canada. Canadian Armed Forces. Air Command--Biography.  4. Airplanes, Military--Canada--History.  5. Canada--History, Military--20th century.  I. Title.

UG635.C2M35 1992    358.4'3'0922    C92-090542-0

Distributed exclusively in the United Kingdom and Europe by:
Airlife Publications
101 Longdon Road
Shrewsbury SY3 9EB
England
(743) 235651

Distributed exclusively in the United States by:
Howell Press
1147 River Road, Bay 2
Charlottesville, VA  22901
(804) 977-4006

McGraw-Hill Ryerson
Toronto Montreal

# FOREWORD

Canadian aviation enthusiasts are fortunate to have so many talented writers, photographers and artists who dedicate their efforts to our favourite subject. They deserve our encouragement as they capture, in picture and in prose, the magic moments of the fascinating world of aerospace. John McQuarrie is of this number and, in his latest photographic odyssey, he focusses his lens on Canadian fighter aviation since the arrival of the jet age.

Each facet of aviation offers its own appeal. It requires no bias, however, to acknowledge the unique fascination and the glamour of the fighter as it stretches the limits of man and machine while forging an alliance between them. The combination of sleekness, at times beauty, with raw power and a sense of imminent danger is hard to match in any other field of endeavour and will never lose its mystique.

Of necessity, John's coverage of earlier aircraft relies on other sources. Several of these aircraft, such as the Sabre, CF-100 and CF-104, have been the subject of books dedicated to them alone.

It is with the CF-18 that his own artistry is most evident, particularly as he covers such major events as the Gulf War and Exercise Maple Flag. The latter offers him the opportunity to add an international flavour; and, if the photographs don't say it all, then the personal insights accompanying each subject ensure that the picture is complete. Recognizing that the aircrew tend to get all the attention, John has taken pains to document the contribution of the many others without whose skills the weapons would not reach the target.

This book will be treasured by young and old alike. The latter will recall their own day in the sun while the former aspire to share those wonderful experiences of flush-rivetted flight. Today's fighter community will find itself reflected, as it should, as a worthy standard-bearer for those who have gone before and for those who will follow. To John McQuarrie and Dave O'Malley I extend, on your behalf, a sincere "Well Done".

LGen David Huddleston
Commander, Air Command

# INTRODUCTION

Their squadron, their airplane, their groundcrew and their performance are all the BEST! If, in all the world's air forces, there are perhaps a total of a thousand fighter squadrons then this assertion will surface a thousand times. Whether it's Nellis, Coltishall, Kubinka or Cold Lake - just stop the first guy you see with wings and ask him where the best fighter pilots live. Arrogant? Obsessed with winning? Brutally intolerant of weakness? You bet! Because, since the business of aerial conflict was born at the dawn of the century, the great fighter pilots have come from a remarkably similar mould. Being the best is what drives them.

This book focusses on Canadian fighter pilots beginning in the years following World War II as the de Havilland Vampire ushered them into the jet age. We will take you quickly through the Golden Age of the legendary Canadair Sabre and on to the Century series which includes the Canadian designed CF-100, the CF-101 Voodoo, and the classic CF-104 Starfighter. For those of you who note that this part of the tour is all too brief, we refer you to the many superb books from the pens of Larry Milberry and David Bashow. You may also want to learn about the Royal Canadian Navy's Banshee, Canada's only carrier-based jet fighter. This is the focus of the latest work by Carl Mills.

Our move to the present day Canadian Air Force begins with a glimpse at the process of training fighter pilots. Then it's on to a tour of the three bases where Canadian Air Force fighter squadrons live. Sadly for the pilots and ground crews who looked forward to Germany, but happily for humanity as it signals the encouraging beginning of a more peaceful world, the Canadian base at Baden-Söllingen will be closed by the time this book comes off the press. The Cold War is over and the peace dividend will be cashed in.

The CF-18 Hornet is Canada's front-line fighter and this beauty will dominate the pages of this book. But it will not be just cold steel. You will see a lot of people herein. While many of them will be pilots you will discover that it is the ground crews that keep the jets flying. In their own words you will learn a little something about their thoughts and the way they go about their business When a particular story is taken from one person's experience his name will appear at the end. If it is a compilation of several peoples' words the piece will be signed off by a simple job title. And if we lifted it from another book that too will be so indicated. Otherwise there will be no captions in the body of the book. But you will find many of the images captioned in a special section at the back.

The world of the fighter pilot is big, dynamic and stunningly beautiful so the emphasis is on the imagery. The words are there to season and compliment the photographs. So, if there's no questions, strap yourself in tight, light the burners and hang on. It's a great day to go flying.

John McQuarrie

**VAMPIRE**

For the new peacetime RCAF the introduction to the jet age came with the purchase from Britain of 90 de Havilland Vampire fighters. To pilots seasoned on Spitfires and Hurricanes this little airplane took some getting used to. The following is an account of a typical introduction:

"I suggest you familiarize yourself with the cockpit a bit - not much to it you know - then I'll give you the exam and off you go. Splendid day for it, what?"

As I sat in the cockpit "just poking around" it occurred to me that the prospect of flying the Vampire without the benefit of dual instruction did not exactly fill my heart with joy. I found the Vampire to be the most unlikely looking aircraft I had ever had the misfortune to encounter. It appeared to me that the designer had made the wings too short, the cockpit too small and had put the engine in the wrong place. Notwithstanding the foregoing, my greatest concern of course was that the bloody thing had no propeller - in my estimation, a very serious oversight.

I wrote the exam and to my great dismay found that every time I made an incorrect response, my two and a half-ringed friend would suggest another response, almost invariably the correct one. His interference was carried to the extent that after he had corrected the document, he was in a position to say that I had just squeaked through with a ninety.

Hon Col Al Gamble
Courtesy of *Airforce* Magazine

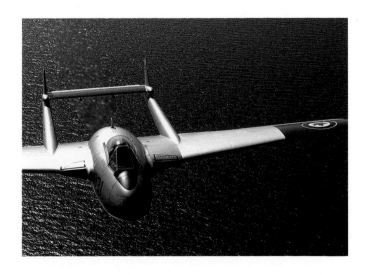

# F-86 SABRE

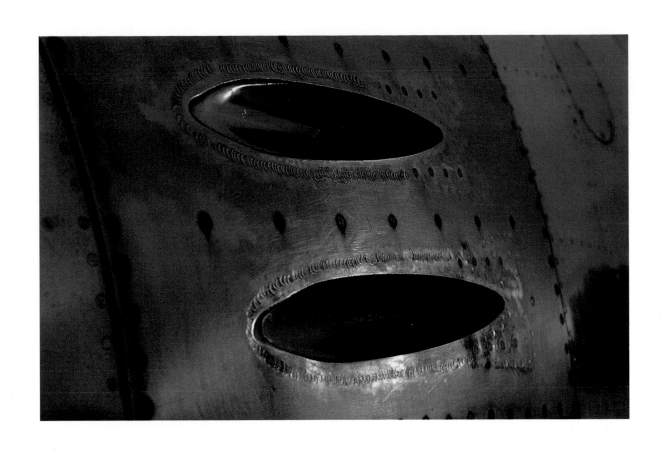

The Sabre, designed by North American Aviation in California just after the war, was destined to become the classic fighter of the jet age — what the Camel and Spitfire were in earlier days. It came along just in time too. As North American and the US military were making major design decisions, such as whether or not it should have a swept wing, the Soviets were pushing ahead with their own fighter, the MiG-15. The MiG got into the air in July 1947, several months ahead of the Sabre, and when revealed as a swept-wing design, fully justified the American decision to sweep the Sabre's wings. Before long these two impressive steeds were doing battle over the Yalu in Korea.

**"Before long
these two
impressive steeds
were doing battle
over the Yalu
in Korea."**

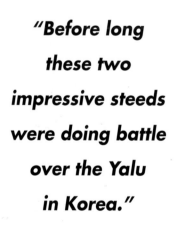

Adapted from: ***Canadair Sabre***
Larry Milberry, CANAV Books

DND

Soon after the Korean War broke out in June, 1950 the RCAF made its primary transport squadron (426) available for United Nations service. Not long after, RCAF fighter pilots were taking exchange postings with USAF wings in Korea. The first of these was F/L J.A. Omer Levesque. He trained on the F-86 in Langley, Virginia and when the unit went to Korea, Levesque was with them. On March 31, 1951, Levesque was escorting B-29 bombers on a raid along the Yalu when his formation was attacked by MiG-15s. Omer got on the tail of the MiG leader, following him down in a spiral dive to 17,000 feet where he managed several hits on a difficult deflection shot from 2000 feet. A second, longer burst from closer in was enough to send the MiG down where it exploded in flames. Levesque thus became the first Commonwealth pilot to make a kill in jet-to-jet combat. Flying Spitfires in World War II, he had made only four kills, one short of the coveted ace status. So this victory held double satisfaction.

S/L Andy MacKenzie was the only RCAF pilot shot down in Korea. He was a seasoned fighter pilot with 8-1/2 wartime kills while flying Spitfires. On December 5, 1952, MacKenzie was on a mission (his fifth) flying No. 2 to Maj Jack Saunders. Near the Yalu, a swarm of MiGs was spotted. The MiGs attacked, and MacKenzie and Saunders became separated. In the ensuing melee, MacKenzie's Sabre was shot to pieces, apparently by one of his squadron mates. There was nothing to do but eject, and within minutes MacKenzie had been captured. He was to remain a POW for two years, spent mostly in solitary confinement.

Canada's leading Korean Sabre pilot ace was F/L Ernie Glover. After flying Hurricanes and Typhoons during World War II and spending two years as a German prisoner of war, Glover served as one of the 22 RCAF fighter pilots to see action in Korea. With three confirmed MiG 15s destroyed and another three probables F/L Glover was awarded Canada's only 'peace time' Distinguished Flying Cross. He was also awarded the USAF Distinguished Flying Cross.

While it is acknowledged that the MiG-15 was superior to the F-86 — it could fly higher and faster — the Sabre pilots had the decisive advantage. They were vastly superior pilots. Many were leading wartime fighter pilots, and it had only been a few years since they had last seen combat. Except for their Russian advisers, the Koreans and Chinese had little experience flying anything, anywhere, let alone jet fighters in combat. The experience level of the Sabre pilots was responsible for their kill ratio of 14 to 1 over the MiGs.

The Sabre soon joined the RCAF, whose top command was determined to enter the postwar era well equipped. In the day-fighter realm, no better choice could have been made. Canadair quickly went to work mass producing Sabres, and adding improvements along the way. From the initial order of 100 machines for the RCAF the company would go on to build a grand total of 1815 Sabres. In the following decades for thousands of Canadians the best years of their lives would be their Sabre years — building, maintaining and, above all, flying this all-time beauty. With a Canadair-built F-86 strapped to his backside, there was no happier or more confident fighter pilot. In those golden years the RCAF had a total of 12 Sabre equipped fighter squadrons. Year after year in the fifties and sixties, Canada's Sabre pilots would walk off with NATO gunnery trophies. There can be little doubt that the presence in Europe of the RCAF Sabre squadrons had a sobering influence upon those behind the Iron Curtain.

# CF-100 CANUCK, "CLUNK"

In service for over 30 years, the Avro CF-100 twin-jet interceptor was one of Canada's great aviation success stories. It is the only Canadian-designed fighter to go into mass production. Known officially as the Canuck and unofficially as the Clunk, the Lead Sled, the Aluminum Crow and other endearing if sometimes unmentionable names, the CF-100

was once a familiar sight in Canadian and European skies. With its Orenda engines housed in bulky fuselage-hugging nacelles, it was a distinctive looking aircraft. Beside today's supersonic fighters it looks positively archaic. Ironically, after many years as an air-interceptor the Clunk found employment in the electronic warfare environment where it reversed roles, playing the enemy bomber it had hunted for so long.

But the intercept role was the Canuck's raison d'être. As a brand new pilot or navigator, fresh from the basic Wings Course, you would report to an OTU (Operational Training Unit) and in 13 short weeks become qualified to defend Canada from a Soviet air attack. The Cold War was in full swing in those years and it was a common occurrence for CF-100 crews to be scrambled on a winter night to intercept an unidentified radar target in the far north. It would go something like this:

**"Leopard Red Section Scramble... Leopard Red Section Scramble. Vector 360, maximum angles. Contact Cupid channel 21."**

*"Cupid Control—this is Leopard Red Leader on Channel 21."*

**"Roger Red Leader—we have an unknown target for you at 150 miles, heading 180 at 40,000 feet. Maintain heading 360, and report**

**level at 40,000 ft."**

*"Cupid—Red leader is level at 40,000 ft."*

**"Roger Red Leader—you are on your displacement vector, your target is at 11 o'clock—range 100 miles—your attack vector will be 270—the target will be crossing starboard to port, tracking 180 level. Your next vector will be your attack vector for an identification pass."**

*"Roger, check."*

**"Red Leader—this is your attack vector. Turn port onto 270. When steady your target will be at 45 starboard—range 30 miles."**

*"Cupid—Red Leader steady 270, searching starboard."*

**"Red Leader—your target is now 45 starboard, 25 miles."**

*"Roger Cupid. We have him in radar contact, 45 starboard at 24 miles and will carry out identification pass."*

**"Roger Red Leader—Cupid standing by."**

In Canadian airspace these intercepts always turned out to be airliners off their planned course, but these young men could not know, for certain, that this would be how it would turn out. There was always a chance that, instead of the TCA or BOAC logo they expected to see on the tail, they would encounter an airplane with no lights and a big red star. On that cold winter night, events like the Cuban Missile Crisis were still in the future. Nor could they fore tell that in a little over 30 years the Cold War would be over and we would be the winners.

Adapted from: *The Avro CF-100*
Larry Milberry, CANAV Books

# CF-101 VOODOO

27

# CF-104 STARFIGHTER

An announcement in the House of Commons on July 2, 1959 selected the Starfighter as the replacement for the Canadair Sabre. Canadair was awarded the contract to build 200 of the single-seat versions under license from Lockheed. An additional 38 two-seaters would be purchased directly from that company.

When Canada made her decision to procure the CF-104, it was intended for employment as a nuclear strike bomber. The Starfighter's airframe was strengthened to accommodate the stresses of a high speed, low-level environment. The radar was optimized for ground-mapping and instead of the M61 Vulcan cannon, the CF-104 had extra fuel cells installed, increasing the internal capacity by 101 Imperial gallons. These, and various other modifications, combined with the aircraft's small radar signature and extended range made her a very viable weapon in the nuclear climate of the 60s.

Canada was out of the nuclear weapons delivery business by the end of 1971 and the Starfighter was retained in reconnaissance and ground-attack roles. Continuous updates of equipment and weapons systems, together with great ingenuity on the part of the airplane's maintainers, kept her operational for nearly 25 years. It saw Canadian military aviation from post-war technology through several generations of fighter development as a bridge to the present. This long period of service was not without cost. Of the original fleet of 238 aircraft, 110 were lost to crashes with 37 aircrew fatalities.

All those personnel involved in the CF-104 through the years share a common place in aviation history. Time has already entrenched the Starfighter as a classic aircraft. It is for the spirit of the 104 era that man and machine are still remembered long after the smoky silhouette and the sound of those J-79 engines are gone from the skies of central Europe.

Adapted from: *CF-104 Starfighter, 1961-1986.*
Neale M. Nowosad
A CF-104 Pilot

# TRAINING

# T-33 SILVER STAR, "T-BIRD"

TO JETTISON CANOPY
PUSH YELLOW T HANDLE FWD

T-Birds have a long and distinguished history with the Canadian Air Force. After serving for many years as a primary jet trainer, they went on to perform in a variety of roles. Reluctant to completely shed their instructional mission, they found work towing targets for aerial and naval gunnery practice. They are also used as missile simulators. Flown against ships at 400 kts only a few feet off the waves, they act just like an Exocet homing on it's target.

We also use them to calibrate our radar installations at Canadian Forces Bases. As utility transport for parts and personnel, they continue to give yeoman service, all the while supporting the biggest flying club in the Air Force.

We call her the "Humbler" in honour of her tendency to keep us all honest. You can always tell when a guy's not current on T-Birds because with that play in the stick on the roll axis he will be waving good-bye on climb-out. Nothing fancy on the instrument panel. Just a regular old 'stick and ball' airplane with standard flight and engine instruments, an ADF, Tacan, one UHF radio, plus guard. And a big old Rolls-Royce jet engine back there that's been doing just fine, thank you, since the early fifties.

Each time I climb into a T-Bird I haven't flown, I check the little plate that tells when she was built. I found one that was just four months younger than I am.

A T-33 Pilot

Our training here is roughly the equivalent of the first half of a private pilot's license in the civilian world, but I've seen guys with commercial pilot's licenses dropped from this course. They call it CT or Cease Training and, to a student pilot, there is no more dreaded phrase in the English language. The standards and rates of progression are unbelievably high, but the reasoning makes sense. Our instructors always say that, given enough time, they could teach a monkey to fly. But they want only the absolute best people to go to jets at Moose Jaw - pilots who can learn fast, make decisions quickly and handle pressure. They would rather CT ten good candidates than let an average one slip through, so they go about their task ruthlessly.

They tell us that during World War II, Canada, through the British Commonwealth Air Training Plan, trained 155,000 air crew for Allied air forces. Standards were high then, and I guess they don't see any reason for things to change. Their attitude seems to be that if you are going to teach people to fly they might as well be good at it.

One of my earlier trips is a perfect example. On leave, before coming to Portage, I did ten hours of dual instruction at my local flying club and I figured I was ahead of the game. My first few trips went great, but on this particular flight I was told to climb out at 90 kts. I felt I was close enough holding 88 kts with everything else pegged. I was wrong. The instructor hooked me with a cold stare and advised that it was bad enough I was not at the requested airspeed but, even worse, was the fact that I knew I was 2 kts under and had done nothing to correct it. As I was absorbing that slap he pulled the power on me and things really started piling up. My landing was so bad the ground crew asked my instructor if he wanted to call the MPs and have me charged with attempted murder. When we have one of those flights where the brain overloads and wants to lock up we call it "havin' a helmet fire".

MUSKETEER

**Boost Check, Change Check-Check, Rich-Hot-Both, Try Start, No Start, Mayday-Mayday-Mayday, DAL Transmit on, 3 Off, 2 Off, Brakes Off, Harness Tight, In We Go...**

Musketeer Forced Landing Check

But I know I'll make it to Moose Jaw. I've learned from my mistakes and I can do it. And I've had my dunk in the tub right out there on the flight line. That comes right after you solo and it's the best bath you will ever have. Even in February. So now it's five more tests and I'm on my way to where I've always wanted to be — fast with a mask and upside down.

A Student Pilot
Musketeers

ircrew Selection in Downsview, the officers course in Chilliwack, language school in St. Jean, mark time waiting for courses in several places, then Musketeers in Portage and, finally, Moose Jaw and jets! And the pressure point was always the same — make the grade or you're out. Even flying the Musketeers was considered the last part of the selection process. The pressure here is, in many ways, even more intense but there is one key distinction. Now they are finally trying to make pilots out of us instead of trying to get rid of us. Feeling this makes all the difference. Now I am not the only human being on the planet that wants me to leave here wearing wings.

A Student Pilot
Tutors

*"Now they are finally trying to make pilots out of us instead of trying to get rid of us."*

TUTOR

# CF-5 FREEDOM FIGHTER

The business of piloting fighters begins here at Cold Lake. We use the CF-5 as a lead-in trainer for the CF-18. From *Moose Meadows* our graduates cross over to the other side of the field where they strap on the Hornet and begin the advanced phase of fighter training. These two phases take the student a little over a year to complete.

The average group will be about 60 per cent new pilots fresh from their Wings Course on Tutors at Moose Jaw with the remainder coming from other branches of the Air Force. We spend the first three months on basic conversion, teaching them to fly the F-5, while the last four months are devoted to teaching them to actually fight with the airplane.

The first phase focuses on learning the aircraft's systems, and then it's on to clear hood, instruments, aerobatics, formation flying and low-level navigation. The CF-5 is a pretty basic little airplane. That means no fancy radar or computers so jettin' along 250 feet off the deck at 450 kts, with a map on your knee, makes for a little added intensity in the cockpit. On these trips the only instrument that will keep me and my student from ending up at the bottom of a smoking hole is the "Mark I Eyeball".

The second phase, employing the jet as a weapons-delivery platform, is were the fun really starts. We teach air-to-ground using 20mm guns, CRV-7 rockets and iron bombs, as well as air-to-air with guns and heat-seeking missiles. In the air-to-air environment, a student's first six trips are BFM (Basic Fighter Manoeuvering). Then he moves on to what he has spent the last two years of his life preparing for — ACM (Air Combat Manoeuvering). He will begin with what we call 1-V-1 neutral which means he will fly beak to beak, one versus one, against an IP (Instructor Pilot). When they pass each other the IP will call, "Fight's On" and they'll crank and bank for position. In this way neither pilot has any angle or energy advantage over the other at the merge, the point at which they actually pass each other and begin the engagement. This will be followed by the more complex 1-V-2 and 2-V-1 offensive and defensive fights.

One thing I've noticed over the years is the dramatic change in the type of students we're getting in the Air Force today. In the old days fighter pilots tended to be younger, single and a little on the cowboy side of the maturity curve. Join a group of students here today in the mess and you would probably find that, if they were not talking flying, they're more likely to be talking mortgage rates or the cost of babysitters than recounting last night's escapades with the fairer sex. You would also discover that, like their predecessors, they have all done well in their past endeavours and have experienced very little failure in their lives. And they all seem to have a very positive, straight-ahead way of doing things.

One thing hasn't changed though. They might be a little more mature today, a little more educated, but — underneath it all — with 450 kts indicated and jet fuel exploding into noise behind them, that sophistication evaporates into balls-to-the wall aggressiveness and you're looking at one formidable individual, totally committed to mastering the skills necessary to piloting a jet fighter.

An Instructor Pilot
CF-5s

**C O L D   L A K E**

Our Fighter Weapons Instructor's Course (FWIC) is the Canadian PHD of tactical aviation. We take one line pilot from each of the eight CF-18 squadrons and put them through a concentrated, three month program. Graduates return to their units and usually take over the squadrons' weapons shop. There they become a pool of knowledge and the hub of tactics. It is the best way to keep the community standards high. To be selected for the FWIC they must be qualified element or section leads, have at least 500 hours on fighters and a year left on squadron. So these are motivated people who already have relatively high skill levels on the Hornet. As an IP (Instructor Pilot), my job is to challenge these guys to be the absolute best they can be. In three months, each one will be surprised to learn just how much he didn't know.

The course focusses on ACM (Aerial Combat Maneouvering) and air-to-ground weapons delivery; the two jobs the CF-18 is equally suited for. A normal day begins with the 5:30AM brief and ends probably around 11:00PM with completed work projects. Students fly in the morning and each 45 minute trip will typically involve at least six hours of preparation. Afternoons are taken up with academics.

But it is the last week when it all comes together. We invite two American fighter squadrons (F-15s and F-16s) up for the graduation phase which will see each of our students leading up to 12 experienced IPs against as many as 25 opposing fighters. It doesn't get any more complex than this.

An Instructor Pilot
Fighter Weapons
Instructors Course

# TECH

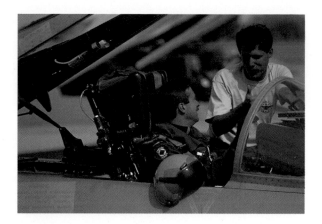

The CF-18 is the most technologically complex aircraft in the Air Force inventory and it takes a lot of highly skilled people to keep it in the air.

It's not for everyone. There's a lot of pressure to keep the jets launching, a lot more hours in the average workweek — what is called overtime in the civilian world — but I am just where I want to be. On the CF-18 we have eight technical specialties. They are: Armour, Avionics, Communications-Radar, Integral Systems, Engine, Airframe and Supply and everybody has to work together to keep the squadron's 12 Hornets in the air. But everyone enjoys the satisfaction that comes from meeting those launch commitments. And the pilots express their appreciation directly to us, which makes a big difference. When I put my rank/first/last on the line saying my part of that airplane will fly, it's a good feeling because I know that when the pilot signs that jet out, first he checks to make sure my signature's there.

A lot of time it feels like we all have two spouses. The person we walked down the aisle with and the Air Force — and often there's a suggestion that it is not necessarily in that order. But demanding work generates a deep sense of satisfaction that can give a person a boost. A boost that follows you home.

A CF-18 Tech

BAGOTVILLE

Just flying the airplane from A to B is easy. The CF-18 is the next thing to a true fly-by-wire aircraft in that it has a fly-by-wire system overlaid on a mechanical one. Flight control information is transmitted electronically from the stick to central computers. These computers then combine the pilot's input with data gleaned from the aircraft's varied sources and feedback loops. The hydraulic servos, which actually move the large control surfaces, are controlled by these computers and are not linked directly to the stick as in most aircraft flying today. In 'auto-flap' mode the computer actually changes the shape of the wing's airfoil at different speeds and angles of attack to maximize performance. But flying the airplane sedately along is not what we're about.

threats. Our CF-18s are capable of carrying up to 17,000 pounds of ordnance, and below 13,000 pounds we can operate throughout our full 7.5G flight envelope. Not bad.

Canadian squadrons are usually equipped with 12 to 18 planes but the basic fighting unit is still the two-ship element. Whenever possible, we prefer to double-up, going to battle in four-plane sections. In 1940 they called it the 'Finger Four' and this deploying of four-plane fighting units still works just fine. And while yes, we have missiles, radar and jet engines — a roll is still a roll and a loop is still a loop. We still have a gun on the airplane to fire on an enemy who is inside the minimum range of our missiles and, like all fighter pilots before us, we still have those little hairs on the back of our necks.

We are on the sharp end. With one movement of my left hand I can select full military power and send my body, and the 35,000 pounds of fire-breathing airplane it is strapped into, hurtling through space faster than a 45-calibre bullet. Through the detents for afterburners or light the pipes and we are supersonic, leaving our own sound behind.

For me, the most appealing part of being a fighter pilot is that we must use both our analytical and intuitive capabilities in concert. Early fighter pilots relied entirely on their eyesight and their intuition to locate and engage an enemy, but radar and the missile age have changed all that. In the CF-18 we have at least 14 different modes of radar to assist us in detecting both airborne and ground-based threats. We have to be able to select and monitor the appropriate systems while keeping track of our fuel, our speed, where we are in space, where our friends are, and where the enemy is, or is likely to attack us from. And we have to continually digest all this information while still flying the airplane. All this is what we call 'SA' or Situational Awareness.

The Hornet is a classic turn-and-burn, weapons delivery platform. It's the fighter pilot's job to employ these weapons. Air Combat Manoeuvring (ACM) or dog fighting is what drives us. In our air combat role the jet is configured with AIM-7M radar-guided Sparrow missiles, AIM 9M heat-seeking Sidewinder missiles, and a 20mm cannon. McDonnell Douglas designed the Hornet as a multi-role fighter which means she excells at attacking both ground targets and air-to-air

So we have the speed and complexity of the information being presented to us combined

with the speed at which we are travelling through space. These elements work together to make the cockpit of a modern jet fighter one of the most demanding office places in the world.

And then there are the G-forces. Fighter pilots in World War II routinely pulled 5 or 6 Gs but in their airplanes the onset was a little slower so they could lighten up on the stick when their vision started to tunnel and in this way avoid the more serious aspects of G-induced loss of control. Put the CF-18 into a brisk bat turn, however, and you can deal yourself a 7 or 8G load instantly. This can mean a correspondingly instantaneous G-induced loss of consciousness with no advance warning. What happens then, is that you literally take a nap. The airplane itself takes over the flying, stops the turn for you and settles down into a nice straight and level 1-G straf target. Your opponent locks on, and you have a fighter pilot's bad day as he guns your brains out.

But being out there on the edge is where we want to be. The CF-18 is a single-pilot airplane. I am the pilot in command. While I alone employ the weapons, navigate and fly the jet, I have the support of hundreds of talented and highly dedicated human beings who work together to make it happen. It has to be the best job in the world.

A CF-18 Pilot

# BADEN SÖLLINGEN

The mess is an oasis to which soldiers have retreated for centuries. Here they acquire a sort of immunity allowing for a more relaxed code of behavior. Relaxed but with structure. What goes on in the mess stays in the mess. For this is truly a private club. It is for members and invited guests only. And every mess observes the same rules, offers the same sanctuary. It is a place where red tape can be cut, or at least trimmed a little. It is a place where you are among friends.

It is also the place to unwind and let off a little steam. The Beer Call on Friday nights is often the scene of lively activity, usually centered around the Crud table. This is a traditional fighter pilot's game played on a pool table but it resembles billiards the way rugby resembles touch football. If the energy generated by these spirited people could be harnessed you could light a major city for a month.

And it is the home of tradition. The beer-soaked antics of a Friday night in the lower bar are in sharp contrast to a traditional mess dinner. Officers are all formally attired in Mess Kit, the military equivalent to black tie. Long tables are perfectly set with fine crystal, silverwear, and bone china. Elegant candelabra and crisp white linen complete the picture. Often a piper will be present and, following dinner, the evening's business will always begin with the traditional: "Gentlemen, the Queen".

Each squadron's Colours are proudly displayed in the foyer of their home station's mess. They carry the squadron's record of Battle Honours and are the focal point of a unit's heritage. One former CF-18 squadron commander was renowned for, amongst other things, encouraging all his pilots to dine together in the mess every Friday. Following dinner they would move to the lobby and, with wine in hand and glasses raised; "Gentlemen, I give you the Squadron's Colours".

# THE MESS

# MAPLE FLAG

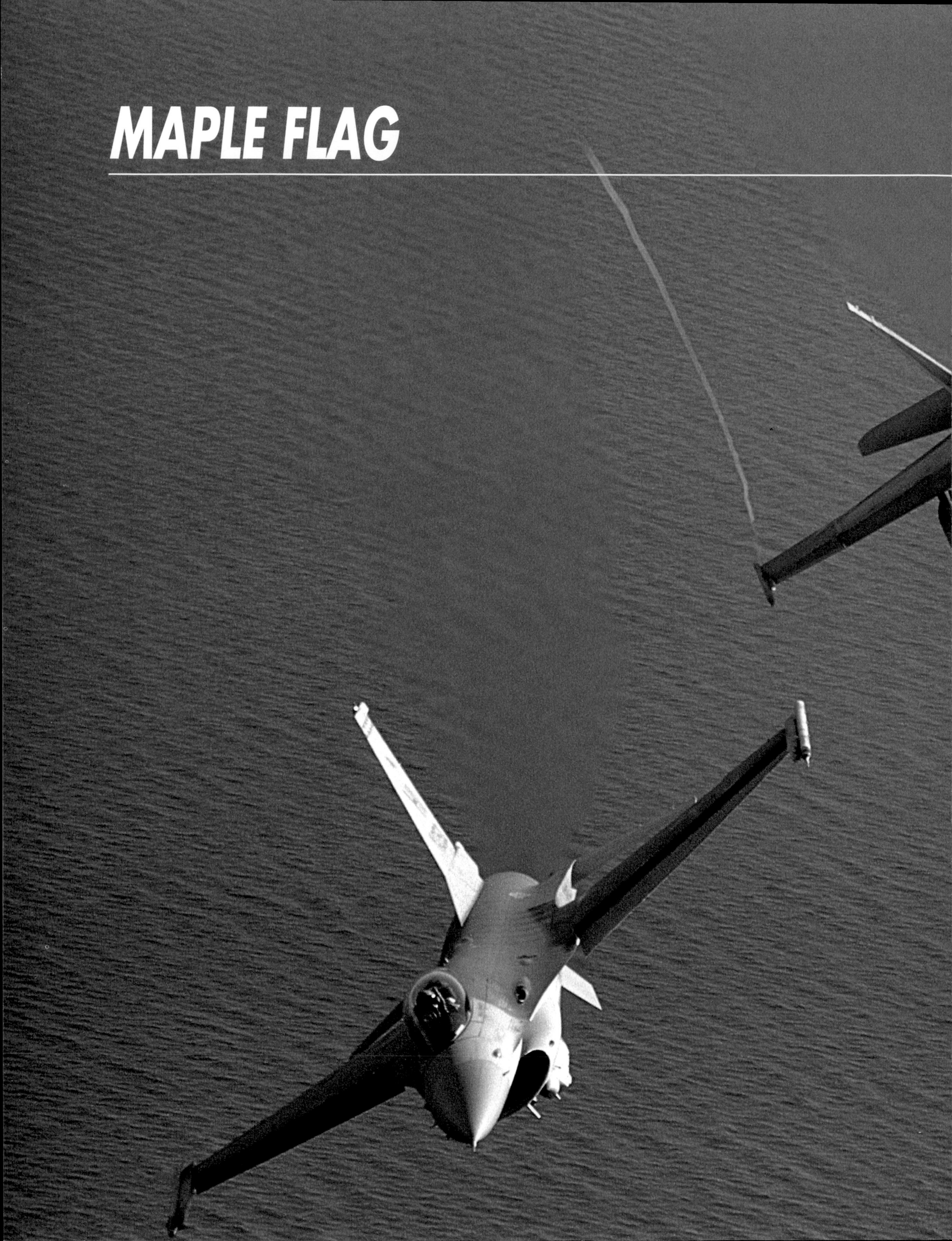

**"It is 7200
square miles
of pure,
turn and burn,
Fighter Pilot
Heaven"**

Since the beginning of aerial combat, one lesson has been learned and relearned. The vast majority of fighter pilots shot down are lost on one of their first ten missions. The purpose of Maple Flag is to give you those first ten trips and to do so in the most realistic, high-threat environment possible in peacetime.

This exercise will simulate the first ten days of a limited conflict. Each day the complexity and intensity will be increased until the end when you will be part of 40 to 50 ship packages out there. You can look forward to opposing fighters, SAMs (Surface-to-Air Missiles), AAA (Anti Aircraft Artillery), com-jamming, AWACS fighter control and a whole whack of adrenalin. Maple Flag is one of the last good deals left. Since 1981, 5800 aircrew and 14,000 support people have launched 36,475 sorties. On a good day you will turn up to 1.5 million litres of jet fuel into flame and noise and you will have a lot of fun in the bargain. You will get out of it just what you put into it.

Unlike other exercises some of you may have participated in, we do not emphasize kill credits here. Lessons learned is what plays for us. Maybe that F-15 guy got you and maybe he didn't but — either way — in that same situation — you won't do that again. That's what counts!

One of the key factors in the success of the 24 Maple Flag exercises run here at Cold Lake over the last 13 years is our Air Weapons Range. It is 7200 square miles of pure, turn and burn, Fighter Pilot Heaven and undoubtedly the best facility of its kind in the world. And there is no civilian traffic so all the airspace is there just for you. But remember that when your radar is indicating

SSGT S WOON
SRA D BROWN
AIC J FINCH

**"If you're number nine on the scene hang on the edge and look for spitters"**

you're 100 feet off the deck don't forget it could be bouncing up off the dirt at the base of a 40 foot tree. Worthy of special consideration are defoliated trees along the tops of ridgelines.

And then there's our Mass Debrief every afternoon at 1700 hours, right here in the Mess. It is a Maple Flag tradition designed to get you all together in one room for a capsule look at the day's battle. One of the benefits of Maple Flag is the interaction within the international fraternity of fighter pilots, so take advantage of the opportunity. It is one more way you can make yourself — and your brothers — better.

Before we get into the detailed portion of death by in-briefing I want to bring up the three most important factors for all of us here. Safety-Safety-Safety! The Rules of Engagement you have all been given lay it all out very clearly and each pilot will digest them and sign a card to that effect before strapping on his jet. Minimums will be those of your own country or ours — whichever are higher. Also, maximum number of jets in a furball will be eight. If you're number nine on the scene hang on the edge and look for spitters. And remember that beak to beak means clear right and nose high goes high. More on this later. So check six, fly smart and fly safe...

Maple Flag In-Brief

110

**Fighter Pilot Heaven...**

**Falcons, Eagles, Rhinos, Aardvarks, T-birds**

**Moose Meadows...**

**Fives, Slufs, Jags, Falcons**

# F-4 PHANTOM II, "RHINO"

Hard to believe the F-4 Phantom flew back in the 50s and she can still hold her own today. Air crews quickly dubbed her the 'Rhino' and 'Double-Ugly' for obvious reasons. I love the intimidating size and bulk of this living legend and that indefinable mystique that is the F-4. Two of the airplanes in our squadron have confirmed MiG kills in the logbooks. Bob Hope once referred to the Phantom as: "the largest distributor of MiG parts in the western world".

We fly with a pilot and WSO (Weapons Systems Officer) or, to use the vernacular, a nose gunner and a tail gunner or pitter in the back seat. As the guy-in-back, my job is to provide the pilot with information on our target, where the threats are and how to defend against them. Having two sets of eyes means we will maintain better SA or situational awareness and SA is what keeps a fighter crew in business.

The Phantom can do everything well with the exception of turning so if we have to battle a *teen* series jet we make him enter our regime and use deception, our extra set of eyes and often greater experience to offset his peformance edge. Phantoms have the same AIM-7s as those guys so we check our radar rather then our 'Six' and try to destroy the other guy's SA early in the fight. We had a particularly good day against the Eagles this morning so we can expect them to pay us a little extra attention tomorrow.

Our squadron is dedicated to training German Phantom drivers and 'Whizzos'. This exercise is sort of their graduation from our advanced, Fighter Weapons Course so it will work out quite well. It's where we put that final Fighter Weapons

**"the largest distributor**

**of MiG parts**

**in the western world"**

Gloss on these guys and they look forward to coming here to Cold Lake throughout their tour with us in the U.S. One of our instructors is a British exchange officer so we like to point out that we have Brits teaching Germans to fly an American airplane.

Here at Maple Flag the program calls for us to switch sides after the first week so we will have the opportunity to fly in both defensive and offensive roles. That is just fine with us because the airplane is quite happy with any type of work it is offered.

A Weapons Systems Officer
F-4 Phantoms

# A-7 CORSAIR II, "SLUF"

## "This unrestricted airspace is a real treat for us Virginia boys"

We call her the SLUF for short little ugly *feller* but appearances are deceiving. She was designed for air-to-mud and carrying iron to the target is her speciality. In short, she is sweet to fly, has high survivability, better than average range — we call it having good legs — and the A-7 was the first computerized airplane. She has a unique, moving map display, whereby maps of the area we will overfly are stored on 35mm film which scrolls by the screen showing us where we are and what's out there on the nose. This makes us very accurate in getting our ordnance on target and is a big help

in our low-level runs into and off a target. We also have a radar altimeter we can pre-set and a computerized HUD (Head-Up Display). The only thing missing is air-to-air radar. We would love to be able to 'see' an attacking fighter but the powers that be probably figure that if they gave us this capability we'd be out there looking for bad guys to fight with all the time.

Here at Maple Flag we will be employed against high value targets and in a CAS (Close Air Support) role. This unrestricted airspace is a real treat for us Virginia boys. Back home we'll be flying along on a mission and when our radar warning gear tells us something out there is trying to spank us all we can usually do is mentally work through the procedure we would employ to defeat the threat. Here we get to actually deal with the diverse threats and most of the time we look like we've just stepped out of a shower rather than the cockpit after a mission. But we love it. It is the kind of flying we all dream about.

The Virginia Militia is an Air National Guard outfit which means most of us fly for the airlines full time, strapping into our SLUFs on weekends and during one and two week exercises like this one. In the old days the Guard was more like a flying club but since the mid-seventies the big change has been a requirement for Guard units to maintain a much higher state of readiness. But it is still one heck of a lot of fun in that we stay together for years and have a lot more experience than most regular air force units. Most of our people have between 1500 and 2000 hours of fighter time.

We'll be transitioning to F-16s before too long, and while I'm looking forward to the Falcons, I will definitely miss my SLUF.

An A-7 Pilot

# F-111 "AARDVARK"

The F-111 began life working for the Strategic Air Command before being transferred over to the Tactical Air Command. At one point they called her the FB-111 because she possessed a unique blend of the best qualities of both a fighter and a bomber. Our guys solved the problem. To us she's an Aardvark or, with due respect and affection, an Earth Pig.

The F-111 is flown by a pilot with a Weapons Systems Officer and was the first sweep-wing aircraft in the air force, in addition to being the first to incorporate a crew ejection capsule featuring air-cushion landing and flotation systems.

We can blow into a target through any weather, over any kind of terrain at Mach 1.2 and never depart from 200 feet above ground. Our Terrain-Following Radar (TFR) allows us to do this hands-off. All we gotta do is get her off the runway and the TFR takes over and drives us to as many targets as we've punched into her computers. It's an amazing piece of gear. The first high-speed penetration you do at night is always fun because you just sit back and trust that when that rate of descent needle is pushing 10,000 to 12,000 feet per minute, you are sliding down one steep piece of mountain in a big hurry and you can't imagine it is only 200 feet underneath you the whole time. Experienced pilots often joke that the only reason they don't do it at a hundred feet is because General Dynamics didn't put a 100 foot switch on the panel. We have a choice of six ride settings at altitude and two down on the deck. Medium gives a soft, ballooning sort of ride while the Hard setting can knock your fillings out. The real secret to the TFR is its swamp gas and mirrors technology. If we want to go a little lower and a little faster we just adjust the angle on the mirror and squirt out a little more swamp gas. Nothing to it.

Part of her ability stems from that variable-geometry wing. It can be swept back from 16 degrees through to 72.5 degrees. Naturally we use the full open, 16 degree configuration for take-off and full sweep for supersonic flight. It is her blistering speed that is her best defence against hostile fighters. This and the fact that we carry lots of gas. If we get into trouble we just light the burners and leave the area of threat at something in excess of Mach 2. Sweep and smoke is the name of this manoeuvre. And there is our bomb in the face or BIF defence as a parting gesture. This means pickling off one bomb and blowing it in the face of a pursuing aircraft — just to give him something to think about. AIM-9s and standard ECM gear round out our defensive capability.

All of this is nice but delivering ordnance on target is the bottom line. We use a radar bombing system for precise weapons delivery. And we are the model of efficiency. While the air-to-air guys can take a whole war to become an ace, shooting down five aircraft, we can take out an entire squadron on a single pass over an enemy airfield. Just ask the Libyans.

A  Weapons Systems Officer
F-111s

# GR1 JAGUAR, "JAG"

Jaguars first came on strength with the RAF in 1973 and we will keep on flying them until the European Fighter Aircraft (EFA) is on line. Right now we don't expect to have the EFA until about 2003, so this airplane doesn't owe us anything.

The Royal Air Force operates Jaguars in a ground strike role but without any dedicated support from sweep fighters or ECM assets. Because of this sort of forced independence we've paid particular attention to the fine art of flying down in the weeds and it has worked out rather well for us. The video tapes from the ground threat sites here at Maple Flag bear this out.

Another trademark of our airplanes is the Sidewinder missile station on top of the wing. We don't do this simply to be different. Our underwing stations are taken up with bombs, ECM and chaf pods and a centre-line fuel tank.

The three remaining RAF suadrons still operating the GR-1A models are all based together at RAF Coltishaw but we get a fair bit of interesting flying. Most of us do a two month stint in Turkey in support of the ongoing Operation Provide Comfort in northern Iraq. In March we discovered a couple of SAM II sites Mr Hussein was building but he was persuaded to remove them after being confronted with our video tapes. We also fly out of Denmark and, of course, some of us get to participate in Red Flag and Maple Flag. All in all, not a bad way to make a living.

A Jaguar Pilot
RAF

**"we've paid particular attention to the fine art of flying down in the weeds"**

**F-15 EAGLE**

Our F-15Es are arguably one of the most capable combat aircraft anywhere in the world. While the standard F-15 is an excellent air-superiority fighter, the Strike Eagle has both air-to-air and air-to-ground capability. So she can attack ground targets and provide her own package protection at the same time.

The other big advantage is the extra pair of eyes in the cockpit. By dividing up the chores our two man crews can concentrate on flying and fighting separately. We like to point out that the nose gunner (pilot) rows the boat and the WSO (Weapons Systems Officer) shoots the ducks.

A Weapons Systems Officer
F-15E Strike Eagles

*"the nose gunner*
*rows the boat*
*and the WSO*
*shoots the ducks."*

# F-16 FIGHTING FALCON

This week our F-16 squadron is working with Canadian CF-18s against the Agressor Squadron's 16s and a bunch of F-15s. The Agressor outfit is trained in Russian fighter doctrine and they fly against us simulating MiG-29s and Sukhoi Su-27s. It got a little confusing until they put red missiles on the Nellis based 16s so we could tell each other apart.

We all love Maple Flag because we get to fly with, and against, a wide variety of aircraft types. This unrestricted airspace here in Cold Lake is great because we can focus all our energy on the mission. No civilian traffic whatsoever. From the time we launch through to bingo fuel and return to base, the only time we talk to air traffic control is when we are twenty miles from touchdown. Also, this exercise is run to simulate a theatre operational base situation which is just the way this unit would go to war. Its undoubtably the best training we ever get.

*"When I want to go there now the airplane takes me there now. To think it is to have it!"*

They call our Falcons the Electric Jets. This is because of their fly-by-wire technology. Electronic transducers translate control pressures to volts. So many volts equals so much hydraulic pressure. Since good old electrons and computers work at the speed of light we get instant response. When I want to go there now the airplane takes me there now. To think it is to have it!

The F-16's side-stick caused a few problems in the beginning. Fighter pilots are used to the stick being between their legs and they're used to it moving. The joke was that the manufacturer had to place it on the side because the jet's cockpit was so small it wouldn't fit in the center. A scant 16

pounds of pressure gives you full deflection. And remember we're talking a 9G airplane here. But the computers will not let the pilot exceed this 9G limit, or whatever angle of attack this translates to. In fact, the original Falcon was so cosmic that the stick on the first series didn't even move. Now this was just too much for boys used to Phantoms and Thuds so General Dynamics built in a quarter of an inch of movement — in four directions. We called this mod the pacifier and it made everybody happy.

An F-16 Pilot

Traditionally, fighter pilots fly combat training missions against members of their own squadron. In the process they become expert at shooting down another pilot that thinks and acts exactly as they themselves do. But aviators from other parts of the world often go to battle under very different criteria. Their tactics can be radically different from ours and that man in the cockpit may have a completely different way of approaching his job.

The Adversary Tactics Squardon of the USAF flys the F-16 but everything we do is designed to simulate the Russian fighter pilot's way of fighting and the way he thinks. Its the old saying; "Know your enemy". As part of the Red Flag organization we fly training missions against American and NATO pilots simulating the tactics a Russian trained pilot might be expected to employ. In addition we attempt to simulate, as closely as we can with our F-16s, the flight characteristics of the MiG-29 an Sukhoi SU-27. Ultimately, we hope that the first time a pilot we have worked with has to fight one of these jets for real, it will be more like his second time. In this business, that can make a heck of a difference!

An F-16 Pilot
Adversary Tactics

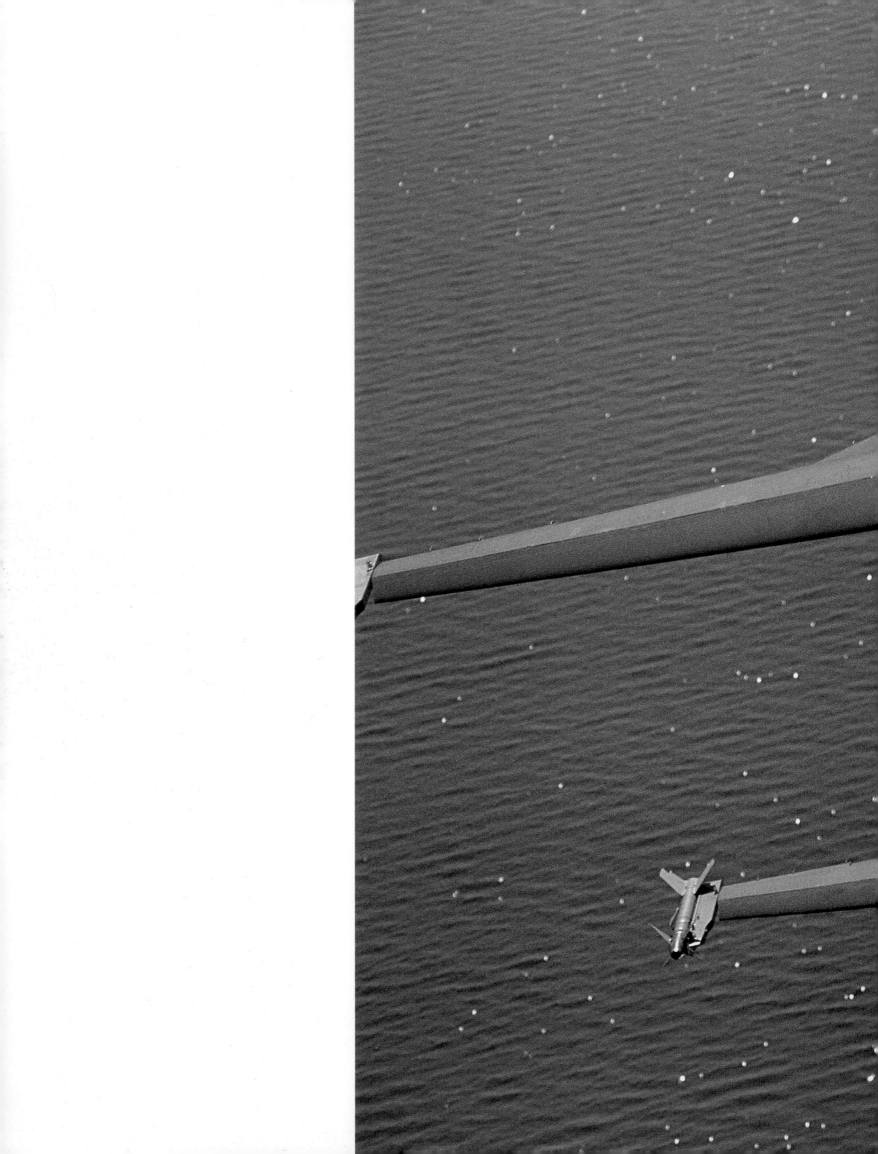

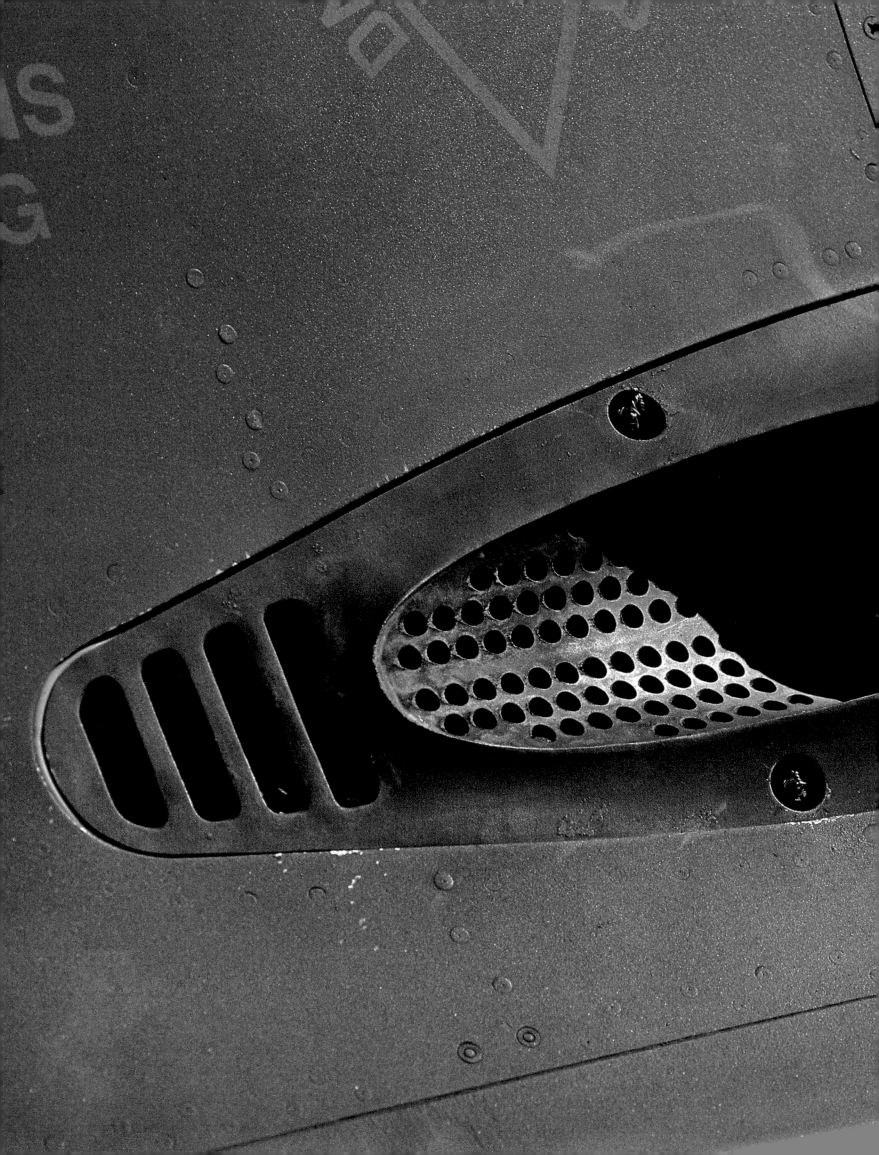

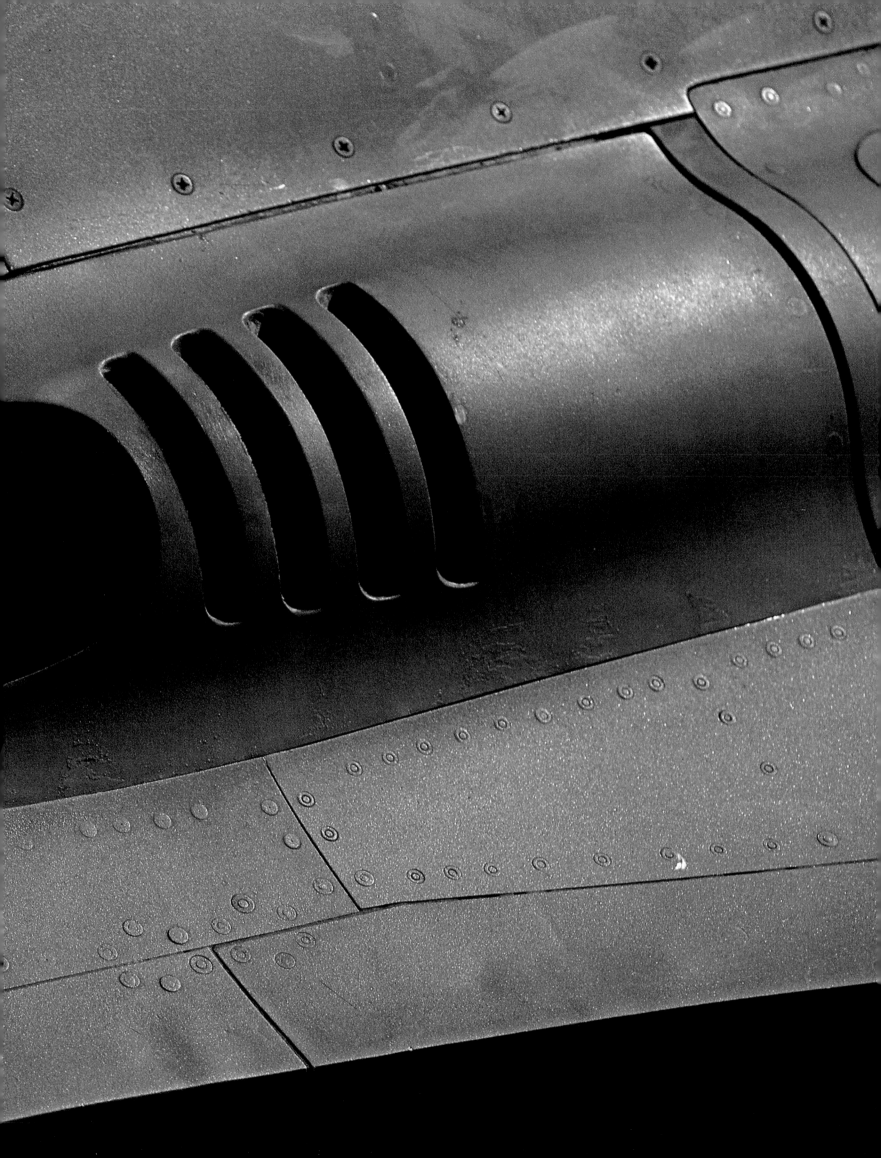

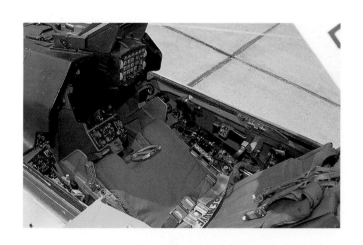

# DESERT CATS

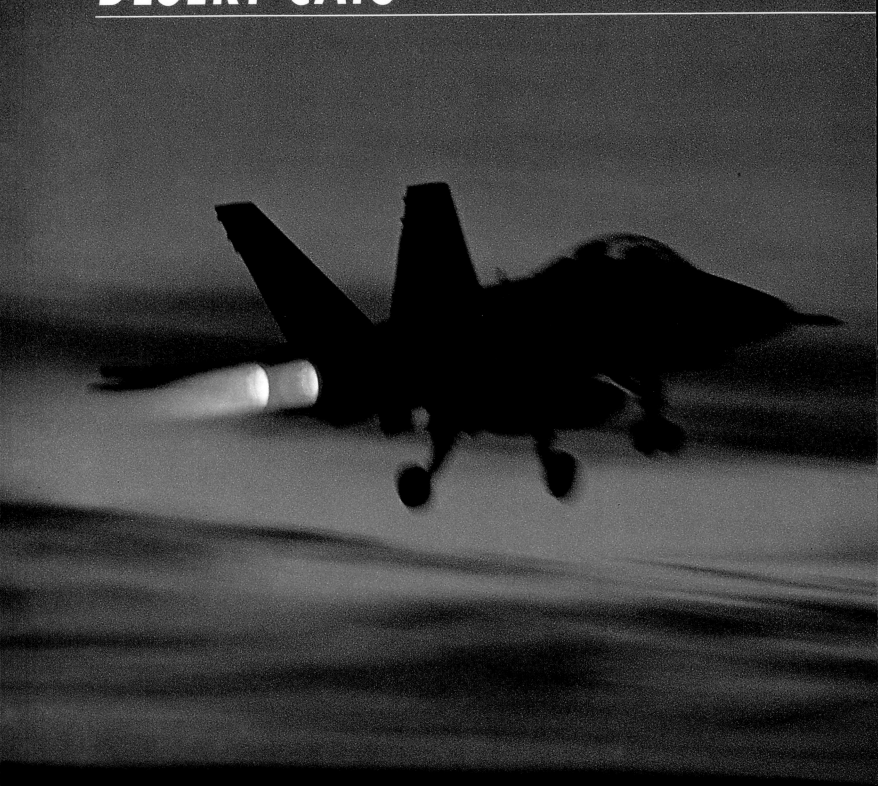

Desert Cats was the name coined to give a separate identity to what was really a composite squadron made up in the majority from Baden's 439 Tigers and Cold Lake's 416 Lynxes. These two squadrons had worked together regularly and effectively in recent years and had an excellent knowledge of each other's habits. This familiarity, together with the spirit and determination of every man and woman assigned to the new organization — and to the 409 Nighthawks, the first Canadian squadron in Qatar — were the decisive factors in their achieving the level of success they did

In the beginning we flew MIG CAPs (Combat Air Patrols) over the Gulf protecting Canadian naval ships. This limited objective was quickly expanded to include all Coalition assets and saw us take up frontline positions well north of the Allied fleet. Often we had to provide 24 hour CAPs which meant having two fighters on station continuously over our assigned sector. This classic positioning as a first line of defence placed us between friendly forces and the source of any potential threat. So our station was always over the Gulf between Coalition ships and the land mass of Iraq and Kuwait.

During the height of the conflict Coalition forces were pumping an average of 2000 sorties a day into the air war so the sky could be a busy place. On clear nights our perch provided a spectacular vantage point from which to witness the Allied blitz on the enemy. The flash of bombs lit up the sky to the north like a thousand thunderstorms. You could see the Scuds rise up from the north and the Tomahawks fly in from the south. In the midst of all this our spins in the CAP orbit would be punctuated by 'commits' on various contacts to positively discern their identity. Some were stragglers which became, for whatever reason, separated from their allied package. Others were battle damaged and required assistance while

some turned back to the north before encountering our protective barrier. CAP required a cool, disciplined approach to ensure that friendlies secured safe passage while no enemy got through.

One week into the war the Cats expanded operations to include the Sweep and Escort role in support of Coalition bombing packages. These Sweep missions saw us go in ahead of bombing packages, far enough in front to disrupt enemy fighters before they had a chance to engage our mud-movers but close enough to ensure spitters, or spin-off interceptors, did not have an opportunity to re-set for a shot at the package.

The Canadian Air Task Group Middle East was based at Doha, Qatar. We were co-located with American F-16s, and Mirage F-1s of both the French and Qatari air forces. Our initial strike escort missions were in support of bombing raids by our F-16 neighbours. On the first sweep I led for them I was surprised to learn that the F-16 bomber lead was an old friend I had flown with on Exercise Maple Flag back in '87.

The Desert Cats had no problem integrating our unit into Coalition strike packages. A large part of the reason for this was joint NATO exercises of recent years where we practiced combined operations just like those we were now running for real. As a result we spoke a common language and, more importantly, we had a high level of mutual confidence, trust and respect. This training dividend would now pay off big-time as we proved the truth behind an old fighter pilot adage: "Train like you fight and fight like you train".

As leaders, we fully expected to be engaged by enemy ground fire enroute to the target. The Iraqis had a surprising array of SAM (Surface to Air Missiles) and AAA (Anti Aircraft Artillery)

Missions flown by Canadians often involved long hours of patrol by CF-18 pairs and would have been impossible without the support of British, Canadian and American refuelers. These gas stations in the sky were always bee-hives of activity as fighters swarmed them hungry for a poke.

On one particularly dark and nasty night my element (two-plane formation) had to hold CAP for five hours instead of the usual three. Our first air refueling was courtesy of a British VC-10. Coming off of him I had to laugh at "The Empire Strikes Back" printed big and bold on his tail. But there were no laughs on the last one.

The final tanker we had to hit was in clouds and, on top of everything, it turned out to be a KC-135. Now the KC-135 is a fine airplane but they normally give their gas through a boom system where an operator in the tanker manoeuvres the boom's nozzle to the receiving jet. On the CF-18 we extend a probe out of our nose and plug a basket that normally is at the end of a 30 foot hose which has a reel-in capability to permit longitudinal movement of the fighter without it falling off the hose. The KC-135's hose is only 9' long and it does not have any retraction capability so it bends in front of the fighter as you poke the basket. This can be distracting as the hose flops around in front of your windscreen. The night before we had three air-raid alerts. Now I had been aloft almost five hours, so the fun was wearing off a bit around the edges. Towards the end of my poke the body started lying to the tired old brain, trying to convince it that we were doing a loop hooked up to that big tanker. It was the beginning of a form of disorientation we call the 'leans'. It happens when the body's balance

*"I had been aloft almost five hours, so the fun was wearing off..."*

system, centered in the inner ear, sends false spatial information to the brain. It took all the concentration I could muster to ignore these human inputs and trust the instruments on the panel that were giving me the true picture of our situation. Still, I was never happier to get my gas and disconnect from an in-flight refueling than on that night.

In the Gulf we used a couple of different formations depending on what type of threats we anticipated. The 'Card' put Lead and Two up front in a Double Attack Spread (basically line abreast with more than one mile between the two) with Three and Four about three miles back and offset to one side. The Card was great for VID situations because the lead pair could make the call and, if declared hostile, the target could be instantly prosecuted by missile shots from the trailers. Unlike fighters of World War II, our formations maintain greater separations to enable us to check behind and below our wingman's jet, as well as making the formation tougher to detect. This also ensures that one lucky shot doesn't take out two fighters.

If SAMs and AAA were players we might go to a 'Wall' with all four aircraft spread out line abreast. This is a more aggressive formation placing all fighters on the same forward firing line. It also has defensive advantages in that it gets all the kiddies across the street at the same time. If we flew over a SAM site with any formation that employed jets in trail, the lead element would activate the ground threat's weapons and the trailers would end up wearing them.

The 'Battle' is like the Wall but sees Lead and Three flying a double attack spread, with their Wingers (Two and Four) swept back on each of them so they are close but still out of the way. Like the Wall, the Battle is offensive in nature but tighter, placing each element in a better position to handle hard turning prior to an air-to air-battle. And there are no tail-end Charlies to eat the SAMs. Also, with sufficient separation between the two elements, it is quite likely an attacking airplane would see and engage only one of the pairs, leaving the second pair free to come around for every fighter pilot's dream shot-the unobserved kill. The Pince was one of my favourites. In this manoeuvre individual elements split to deceive, bracket or force the opposition to choose sides and risk an unobserved entry from the free element.

One of the beauties of the Desert Cat experience was that we always flew with the same four section pilots. We learned in World War II that this pairing allowed members to learn each others moves and timings, making for much more co-ordinated fighting units. This familiarity bred the knowledge and trust required to allow formations to 'Breathe' from one structure to the next as the threats and circumstances changed. This is no

easy task as each formation carries with it a different set of responsibilities or Contracts for each individual member. Weapons employment and threat reaction timing, for example, might be very different between the Wall and Card formations

All of us experienced fear. For the pilots it may have occured as they watched and reacted to smoke trails rising up at them from the ground. Or it would be the moment an unidentified target, closing at 1000 miles an hour, makes an offensive move that means he has seen you. For the ground crew it might have happened as they were startled awake from a deep sleep, in pitch black, to the wail of an air-raid siren and began frantically searching for their chemical suit. The funny part was that, once you got into gear and began dealing with the event, this activity - often very focused and concentrated - left little room for worry. The fighter pilot automatically initiated defensive manoeuvering to negate the missile launch while the ground crew systematically donned his chemical gear and turned to help his buddy. Then, after it was over, you had time to think about just how fragile your comfortable attachments to the world actually were.

If there is one point all of us who were there would now agree on, it would be our admiration and awe for the courage shown by the wives and families back in Germany and Canada. The fast breaking events of the day kept us very busy, but this was not necessarily the case back home. They were witness to the Baghdad fire-fights, listened to incomplete reports of F-18s being shot down and viewed allied POW interviews. New rumours were born every hour. Satellite television technology put the war in all their living rooms, 24 hours a day, live. Often those at home knew more than those of us who were living it. But they had no recourse to effect the outcome and had to deal with a perception shaped by the media and the terror of the imagination. The reality was inescapable but they banded together and supported both the troops and each other. They were the unsung heroes and we love them for it.

Maj Russ 'Coop' Cooper
Deputy Commanding Officer
Desert Cats

There is a phrase that we, as fighter friends, casually toss off to one another as we walk out to go flying. It is said at the bar, to a departing drunk's back, or during a crud match at a hazy 1 o'clock in the morning. During peacetime, which has been a long time in our Air Force, it has lost some of its cold, hard logic, (diluted by the fact that ignoring its warning could only bruise your ego). It was first known in the Great War as 'beware the Hun in the sun', and it's been said in different ways by fighter pilots ever since. I don't know how many times I have said it, but this is the first time I have said it and really meant it — — — "CHECK SIX"!

Craig 'Richmo' Richmond
Former CF-18 Pilot
Writing to a friend in the Gulf.
Adapted from: *Desert Cats*
Fortress Publications

The big thing is to have the required number of serviceable jets for the day's 'program'. In peacetime Canadian fighter squadron maintainers work two shifts. The day shift deals with problems that develop during flying operations and the night shift takes over at 4:00pm. The night crew leaves only after ensuring enough jets are ready for the next day's flying. A unit's success is measured on its record of serviceability, expressed as a percentage of aircraft it keeps mission-ready. Most of the year we put in 40 to 50 hours a week and, like our civilian counterparts, get most weekends off.

A lot of this changed when we deployed to the Persian Gulf. There you were either day or night shift and that was how it would stay for the duration. You worked seven days, 12 hours per day. It worked out to 84 hour work weeks. And that's not counting time spent filling sandbags. The Gulf was also the place to discover just what people were really made of. You could see the guys that were meant to be fighter pilots rather than air show pilots and the people that showed up for sand bag details turned out to be the ones you knew you could count on the most.

If I had to pick the one thing that stands out most in my impressions of the whole Gulf experience it would be the unbelievable spirit of co-operation that gripped everyone. The old phrase; 'It's not my job' was never even thought of, much less spoken. Sure each of us had our own particular trade qualification on the CF-18 but the moment anyone needed help, in any area, there was a bunch of people right there to give it. So you might have armourers helping with a start check or engine techs helping to load bombs. As long as there was one person qualified to sign the work off

everybody was happy. Because of this the Desert Cats enjoyed an enviable 100 per-cent mission serviceability. Not bad! It was just the way I had always imagined the Air Force was meant to be.

The climate was a little different from what we were accustomed to in Cold Lake. But our jets seemed to like the hot dry air well enough. In fact it was really hard to believe we had deployed with some of these same machines in arctic conditions. The sand played havoc with items like avionics but, strangely enough, the engines thrived on the stuff. The normal accumulation of creasote in the back end never happened. And the titanium compressor blades lost a bit of surface texture but continued to perform perfectly. It kind of reminded me of my self-cleaning oven back home.

Another amazing aspect of the war was the truly massive support we received from all corners. The first thing that became evident to us was that every single member of the Canadian Armed Forces was putting our needs ahead of their own. If we requested a part and the only one in existence happened to be in Comox, it would be loaded on the next Hercules flight out. No problem. Then there was the avalanche of letters and parcels from complete strangers all over the country. To say we were overwhelmed is an understatement. It was simply great and I wish we could write every single Canadian that responded so generously and tell them how much it meant to us.

To sum it all up, I'd have to say that I wouldn't ever want to do it again but I wouldn't trade it for a million bucks either.

A CF-18 Tech
Desert Cats

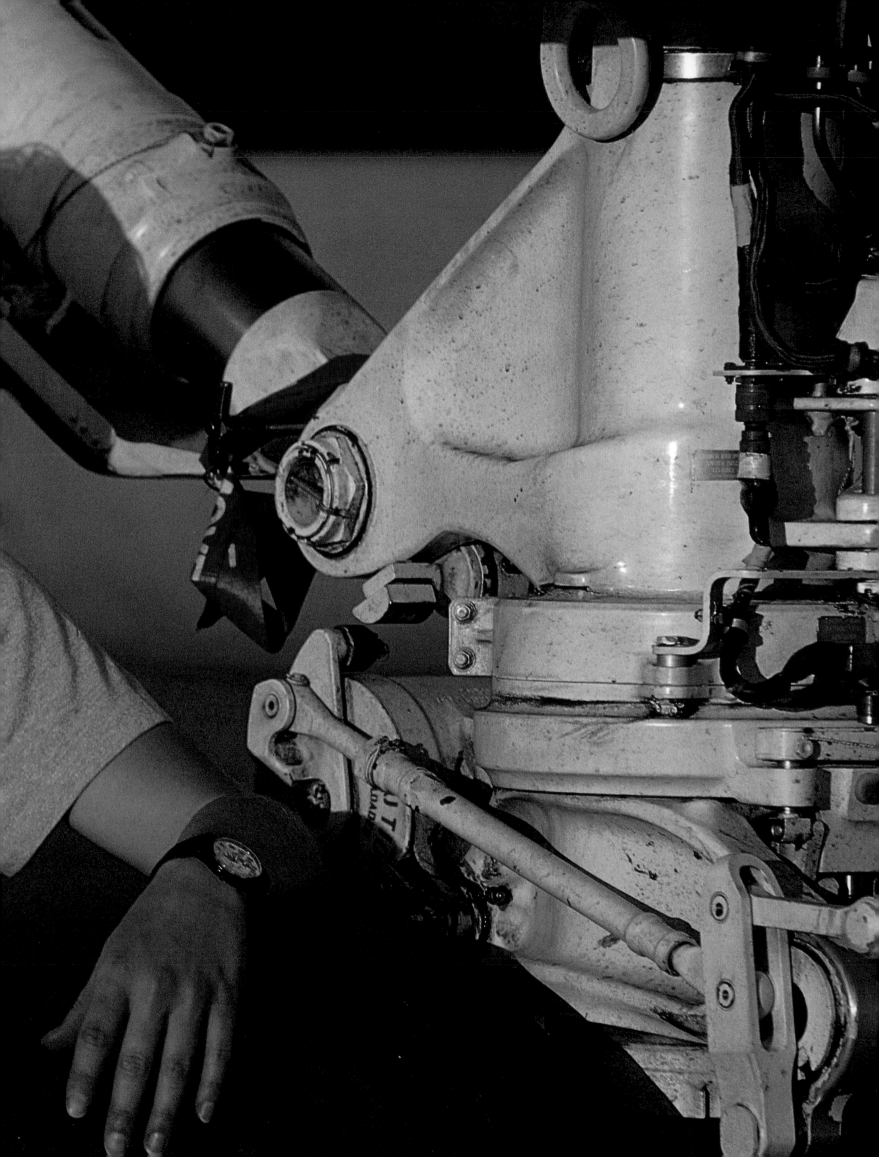

I woke up early, before the alarm, on the 25th of February. As I sat in bed, thankful that there had been no air attacks the previous night, it struck me that the birds don't sing in the morning here. Perhaps it was a sign of what was to come.

Today's mission would be different. Up to now we had been flying MIG SWEEP and Strike Escorts and our orders were to fire only in defence of ourselves, or our package, if enemy fighters entered our assigned piece of sky. This never happened. Now, rather than sweeping a sector to ensure it was safe for someone else to attack ground targets, we had finally received clearance to mount our own air-to-ground STRIKE missions. Apart from putting Canadian fighters in an offensive posture, this change meant we would be going directly into the surface-to-air missile (SAM) threat area that — until now — we had so carefully avoided.

The target we were tasked to bomb was an Iraqi artillery position deep inside Kuwait. We had briefed the tactics thoroughly the night before and knew the weapons we would employ. Each of our four Hornets would carry eight MK82, 500 lb, high explosive bombs, for a total of 32. And we would have no dedicated air escort. The CF-18 was designed to retain a potent air-defensive capability even when assigned to a ground-attack role. We would rely on ourselves for our own package protection.

**"I dipped my wing in time to see all eight bombs gliding swiftly through the air like a school of hungry piranhas searching for their prey."**

The planning sequence that morning went exactly as it had a hundred times before in training. We received our intelligence briefing, planned the attack, and dressed for the mission. But today we all carried extra clips for our 9mm pistols because we knew we were going deep. And we removed all insignia from our flight suits. This was serious. I took the opportunity to read a letter from my wife that I had received the day before but had saved for this moment. In it, she told me that she was scared, but that she believed in me. I knew I wouldn't let her down.

As I approached my jet and greeted the groundcrew who had so diligently prepared her, I noticed the ominous look of the eight 500 pounders that broke her sleek lines. A Sidewinder on each wing-tip and the two Sparrow missiles tucked into place underneath completed the ordnance package on the air-to-air side. She was ready for what I would soon ask of her and today that could well be everything she was capable of giving.

Hornet 01 Flight taxied out to position for take-off. Lodgepole leading, Bambo in the number two slot, Rigs as number three and myself, Smak rounding out in number four. Holding on the button, I watched as one by one they lit their afterburners and broke away from the earth's pull into the hot desert air. As I selected full burner and accelerated down the runway I noticed immediately that my machine didn't leap into the air with her usual enthusiasm. It was as if someone had replaced my Ferrari with Dad's Buick. Although we had pre-briefed it, the realization struck home that if bounced by enemy MiGs, these heavy bombs would be the first things to go.

After about 45 minutes, flying above a blinding sandstorm that covered most of Saudi Arabia, we rendezvoused with the tanker. Today it was our own Boeing 707, Husky. It was somehow comforting to slide up to this familiar old friend, topping up our tanks from her two wing-tip hoses. As we departed the tanker track and turned toward our push-point in hostile territory we heard a call of "Good hunting boys" from the Husky commander. We hoped there would be.

Selecting full military power, the section began a climb to altitude, always ensuring that we had enough airspeed to defend against any SAM that might leap up to greet us. As we approached the Kuwait border, there was an overcast layer topped at about 20,000 feet so we knew we would have to bomb through cloud. The CF-18 and her onboard systems are more than capable of this task.

We pressed with the planned route, armed our weapons and contacted the Airborne Command and Control Center (ABCCC) at the designated point. ABCCC gave us a FLOT (Forward Line of Own Troops) update and it was immediately apparent that the FLOT had advanced so dramatically our assigned target was now in

208

friendly hands. As we realized this ABCCC came back with…"Hornet 01 flight, standby". Immediately the thought of having to drag two tons of iron bombs all the way home raced through my mind. I wanted desperately to contribute directly to the land battle that was going so well. After several long minutes ABCCC contacted us again…"Hornet 01 flight you are cleared to contact Rebel on TAD 25 for target information" Lodgepole switched us over to the appropriate frequency and checked us in… "Hornet 01 flight check left…two…three…four". Then Rebel, a Forward Air Controller (FAC) gave us a target about 90 miles deeper than we had planned for. We crunched out the fuel required and Lodgepole decided we could make it. The reply came back: "Roger, Hornet 01 this is Rebel, your target is armoured vehicles assembling and moving north" in support of the Iraqi defense. I programmed the new target data into my INS

(Inertial Navigation System) and it seemed to take us only a brief minute to cover the distance. About 30 miles back from the target, we took turns going 'heads down' and selecting our radar to the air-to-ground mode. When Rigs called "heads up" it was my turn. It took only seconds to switch the radar from an air-to-air display, looking for enemy fighters, to an air-to-ground display looking for ground targets. I couldn't believe my eyes! The scope immediately broke out a column of vehicles about 6 km long. Expanding the radar picture to take a closer look, I centered my target acquisition cursor over the most heavily concentrated area. My heart was pounding in my chest. This was for real! We were in the game!

Because of the cloud, a dive-delivery would not be required so I followed the INS steering cues to the target designated on the radar picture. The system

told me where to place my aircraft in the sky and when to deliver my weapons. All the while I was checking Rigs' Six for possible SAMs since we were deep in enemy territory and their targeting radar had been locking us all the way in.

When I saw the bombs come off Rigs' jet I immediately looked for the release cue in my Head-up Display and there it was. I've never felt so focussed in all my life. I enabled the pickle button to allow the system to release the bombs at the pre-computed point. The aircraft shook violently as the heavy load fell away. I dipped my wing in time to see all eight bombs gliding swiftly through the air like a school of hungry piranhas searching for their prey. No longer burdened by the heavy bombs we climbed higher, to put as much sky as possible between ourselves and the enemy Anti-Aircraft Artillery, as we turned for home. The flight back to Doha was routine, and I felt very relieved that all had gone so well.

That evening I sat outside my trailer under a surprisingly peaceful desert sky, smoked a Cuban cigar that I had been given for just such an occasion and, savouring the moment, re-read my wife's letter.

Capt Gerry 'Smak' MacKinnon
A CF-18 Pilot Desert Cats
Adapted from: **Desert Cats**
Fortress Publications

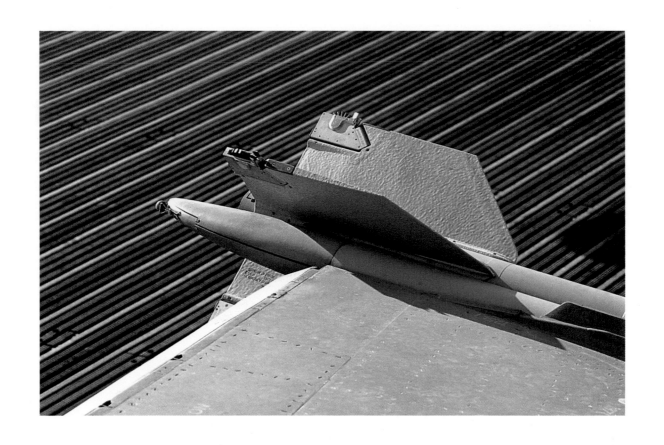

# EQUIPMENT

People viewing my images invariably ask; "What type of camera do you use?" After answering, I am quick to add that the camera body is the least important element in the loop of picture taking. Cameras don't make pictures. Imagination and light make pictures. The camera body is merely a box that will drag film along behind the lens and keep it in the dark except when you click the shutter. All the major brands will yield the same photograph when equivalent light, film and lenses are used. If your camera allows you to set your own choice of aperture and shutter speed, allows the use of flash and has a *depth of field preview* button, you are all set. If you are not clear on this last item, ask the salesperson who sells you film to explain its importance. Spend your money on lenses and film!

All the photographs in this book were taken with Nikon 35mm equipment. I travel relatively light, relying on only four lenses. They are a 20mm 4.5, a 35-70mm 2.8 zoom, an 80-200mm 2.8 zoom and a 300mm 4.5. Camera bodies are two beat up old FMs and an 801 auto-focus. Add a tripod, a couple of polarizers, a pair of flashes with a slave unit, light meter for incident readings, clamp with tripod head, gaffer tape and the kit is almost

complete. All the photographs in this book were shot on Fuji's Velvia (50 ASA) chrome film. No, Nikon and Fuji didn't pay me to say this — but they should have.

The black, egg shaped unit in the photo is a Ken Lab gyro— stabilizer. It screws on to a body or long lens just like a tripod and, after spining up to 25000 rpm, provides incredible stability for hand-held shooting at slow shutter speeds. I can get away with a 60th of a second with my 300mm and correspondingly slower speeds with shorter lenses. So it allows me to hand hold during early morning and late evening shooting when the light is at its best. And remember were talking film speed here of 50 ASA. The other advantage it offers is in the air-to-air environment where vibration dictates the use of higher shutter speeds — 250th in a fixed wing machine and 500th in a helicopter. But shutter speeds of a 250th and up freeze propellers so the airplane looks like it's parked in mid-air, while down around a 60th you get a full rotation of the prop during exposure. This makes the airplane look much more realistic because it shows that the engine is running. About the best way to explain it is that it lets me shoot 50 ASA film in situations that, without it, I would be forced to go to 1000 ASA.

# ACKNOWLEDGMENTS

Cpl Dale Amos
Capt Allan Andrukow
Alain Anka
WO Wes Arnold
MCpl Chuck Arnsten
Lt Paul "Ax" Axelson USN
Capt Paul "Curley" Ayers
LCol John "Chief" Bagshaw
Capt Pat Baisle
Lt Al Baldwin
Capt Todd Balf
Capt Alan "Bam Bam"
    Bampton
Cpl John Barnhardt
F/L Nick Barr RAF
Maj Bunky Barrett USAF
Lt Brooke Bateman
Cpl Jim "Batman" Bateman
LCol Rick Bates USAF
Capt Oliver "O'Man" Baus
Lt Darron Bazin
Capt Bob "Beards"
    Beardsley
WO Beattie
Capt Serge "Budgie"
    Beaulieu
Capt Jeff "Beck" Beckett
Pvt Eric Belanger
Capt Fernand Belanger
2Lt Greg Bend
F/L Derk Bendall RAF
LCol Frank Bernard USAF
Capt George "Chicken"
    Bertrand
MCpl Phil Berube
Capt Dean Besalt
Capt Sylvain Besner
Capt Gregg "Mr Bill"
    Billman USAF
MWO Bob Bissett
Capt Philippe Bleau
Maj Yvan "Bad" Blondin
Capt Ulrich Bollinger
Capt Duane "Booser"
    Boosamra
Michael Bourque
Barry Boyes
MCpl Brian Branch
Capt Bill "Bronco" Brown
1Lt Kevin "Buster" Brown
    USAF
Col Bob Bufkin USAF
Maj Jim Burger
MCpl Dean Burns
Maj Dave "DC" Burt
MCpl Bill Burton
Capt Emile "Cuffs"
    Calderon
Lt Frank Cannon
Capt Dave "Kahn" Carr
    USAF
Capt Doug "Dog" Carter
Capt Chris "Cream"
    Ceplecha USAF

Sgt Brad Chambers USAF
Smitty Chapelle
Cpl Aurele Chevrier
MCpl Bill Clark
Katie Clark
Capt Chris Coates
MCpl Alvin Cole
Cpl Roger Cole
Capt Chuck Collins
LCol Chris Colton
Maj Russ "Coop" Cooper
Capt John Couch
MCpl Randy Court
Capt Rob "Throb" Cox
Becky Cudmore
MCpl Ted Dawe
Capt John Deboer
Capt David "Bambi" Deere
Ptc Rob Dehaan
LCol Dan Dempsey
Capt Pierre "Dez" Desbiens
Lt Bob Destasio USAF
BGen Gordon Diamond
Tim Dube
MCpl Richard Duchesne
Sgt Ade Ducros RAF
Maj Dan Duggan
F/L Dave Edwards
Lt Nigel Edwards
LCol Doug Erlandson
LCol John Evans
Capt Faucher
Cpl Robert Felder
Maj Jeff Foss
MCpl Marc Fugere
LCol Bob Gabor USAF
Ray Gagnon
A1C James Gerhart USAF
Bryan Gibbins
Cpl Dan Globensky
WO Andre Gloutnez
Capt Michel Goulet
Capt Gary "Grabber"
    Grabowski USAF
Maj Steve "Igor" Gregor
    USAF
Pte Dieter Grimes
LCol Ron "Dinger"
    Guidinger
Capt Steve "Hatchet" Hale
Maj Rick Hanna
Capt R.M. "Eddie" Haskins
Maj Al Hawley USAF
LCol Laurie "Hawnski"
    Hawn
Capt Tony Haynes USAF
LCol Tony Haynes USAF
Col Jim Henderson USAF
LCol Csaba "Chub" Hezsely
Sgt Sheila Hiscock
Col D.F. Holman
Capt Pete Holmwood
Sgt Burt Howard
LGen David Huddleston

Sgt Ken Huffman
Capt Rob "Smoke"
    Huguley USAF
LCol D.F. "Yogi"
    Hyghebaert
Capt Gordon Ireland
Col Glen Jepsen USAF
Vic Johnson
Capt Tony Jones
Capt Rick Jones
Maj Charles Joseph USAF
Col Dave Jurkowski
Maj Dave "DW" Kendall
Maj Trevor "Trev"
    Kennedy
CWO Clay Kerry
Capt Paul "Rose" Kissman
LCol Mike "Korn"
    Koerner USAF
Capt George "K9"
    Kramlinger USAF
Capt Jimmy "Bugs" Kyle
Cpl Luce Labadie
PO Mike Labossiere
Lt Serge Lacasse
MCpl Yves Lagimoniere
Maj Bob "Du Lac" Lake
Col Romeo Lalonde
Bill Lamberton
Pte Francois Landriault
MWO J.J. Landry
Ron Lapp
Capt "Bunny" Larocque
Capt "Bingo" Larue
MCpl Andre Laviolette
Capt Claude "Lucky"
    Lavoie
Capt Steve "Sack"
    Le Gassick
Tery Lebel
Lt Duane Lecaine
Capt Tony "Bones"
    Ledsham
Cpl Martin Lemire
LCol Clark "Boss" Little
Don Loney
Capt Michael Lopoianowski
Sgt Hank Lous
Capt Brent Luebke
Sgt MacDonald
Capt Neil MacDonald
Capt Rene MacTaggert
Maj Marcel Major
Maj Michael Maquet USAF
LCol Benoit "Big Ben"
    Marcotte
SSgt Tony Mason USAF
Cpl Francois Masse
Cpl Brooke McCabe
Lt Christine McCarthy
Capt Karen McCrimmon
LCol John McGillivray
Lt Tedd McHenry
Capt Ian McLean

LCol John "J Mac" McNeil
Capt John "Clam" McNeil
    USAF
Capt Francis Mercier
LCol Fred "Moose" Meuller
Capt Bill Michael
Larry Milberry
Maj John Mitchell
Capt Paul "Pitch" Molnar
Sgt Nick Moore RAF
Cpl Michel Morin
Cpl Jeff Morris
F/S Jeff Morris RAF
Maj Bill Motriuk
Alex Moyes Jr.
Pte Rob Muraca
Maj Bob Nagy USAF
Capt Rett "Fig" Newton
    USAF
LCol Pete Nodwell
Maj Jim Nunnallee USAF
Capt Ole Nygaard RDAF
BGen Dave O'Blenis
Lauren O'Malley
Merrill O'Malley
Capt Bob Orme
LCol John Osborne USAF
Stephanie Owens
Murray Palmer
Capt Graham Patrick
Maj Van "Poncho "Peterson
WCdr Bill Pixton RAF
Tom Pollard
Capt Todd Post USAF
Cpl Les Prosser
Capt Hart "Stubby"
    Proksch
S/L John Reeve RAF
Capt Paul "Rigs" Regli
Capt Steve Reitmann USAF
Capt Abbe "Abbie" Resce
    USAF
Capt Jim "Malibu"
    Reynolds USAF
Maj Dave Richards
Capt Claude Robert
Capt Kevin Roberts
Lt Stephen Roberts
Cliff Robertson
Capt Pierre Ruel
Maj Bill "Stiff" Ryan
Maj Veejay Ryan
Sgt Mark Sabad
Maj Brian "BJ" Salmon
LCol Dave Sams USAF
Sgt James Sanford USAF
Cpl Scotty Schubert
Lt Mark Scott
Capt Mike Sejourne
Capt Bob Selleck
Lt Andre Shank
Capt Greg "Shep" Shepherd
Cpl Gary Sideen
Cpl Patsy Slapsys

Capt Todd Smith
Capt Gord Smith
LCol Jim Smith USAF
Capt Bill Snedden
Lt Brent Sparks
Sgt Bill Spellman
Maj Tony Spraggs
Sdt Renaud St. Pierre
Capt Brian "Stoker" Stook
Henry "Gyro" Struck
Maj "Duff" Sullivan
Col Bob Summers USAF
LCol Dennis Tabbernor
F/L Laurie Tallack RAF
Capt Jeff "Ira" Tate
Capt Tom "Jaws" Taylor
LCol Buck Taylor USAF
Capt Yves "YV" Tessier
Capt Yves Therrien
Capt Neil Thomsen
Dave "Air Show" Timms
Capt Ben Toenders
Capt Rick "Ricardo"
    Traven
Capt Sylvain "ST"
    Tremblay
Maj Ed Ukrainetz
Cpl Avril Van Aert
Capt Willem "Rooie" Van
    Gaalen RNAF
Cpl Mario Vedotaw
Cpl Joe Verreault
Capt Marcus "John Boy"
    Walton
Col Mike Wansink
Cpl Mark Wells
Pvt Rob Wengel
LCdr Wally West
Capt Tony White
Maj Bart Wickham
MCpl Louise Williams
Lt Rick Williams
Cpl Robert Williams
Maj Bill Wilson USAF
John "Gentex" Winship
Maj Mike "Trapper"
    Winters USAF
LCol Jim "Wiz" Wisdom
    USAF
Capt Gary Wolver USAF
LCol Barry Wyttenback
    USAF
Sgt Carey Young
F/L Simon Young RAF
MCpl Steve Zabbo
Capt Daryl Zeleny
Capt Dave ZiomehUSAF

# CAPTIONS